Cover photo courtesy of Darrett Sanders.

FOR THE LOVE OF
(or, the roller derby play)
© Gina Femia
Trade Edition, 2018
ISBN 978-1-63092-114-9

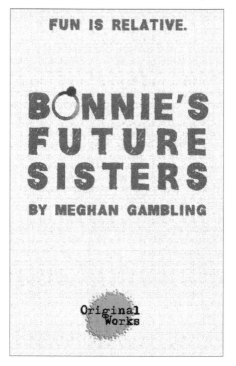

Bonnie's Future Sisters by **Meghan Gambling**

Synopsis: When self help author Bonnie invites Corey to her engagement party, Corey heads to North Carolina to try to rekindle her friendship with her younger sister— only to find that Bonnie appears more excited about her future sisters-to-be, Kayleigh and Larissa, than Corey. Despite Bonnie's best and meticulously planned efforts, her party threatens to be a total bust—especially when one of the sisters goes missing.

Cast Size: 4 Females

FOR THE LOVE OF
(or, the roller derby play)
By Gina Femia

For The Love Of (or, the roller derby play) received its professional premiere at Theatre of Note in Los Angeles, CA, opening on April 26, 2018. Produced by David Bickford, Kelly "Lucretia Hott" Lingen & Jenny Soo. It was directed and choreographed by Rhonda Kohl.

The ensemble was as follows:

Cassandra Blair
Crystal Diaz
Elinor Gunn
Liesel Hanson
Lynn Odell
Alina Phelan
Yolanda Snowball
Jenny Soo
Tania Verafield
Faith Imafidon
Cindy Lin
Nadia Marina
Nicole Gabriella Scipione
Nancy Stone

The production crew was as follows:

Assistant Director: Lauren Smerkanich
Stage Manager: Aaron Saldaña
Assistant Stage Manager: Ellie Chaika
Sound Designer: Gilly Moon
Scenic/Prop Designer: Elizabeth Smith
Costume Designer: Vicki Conrad
Lighting Designer: Rose Malone
Graphic Designer: Maybelle Pineda
Master Carpenter: Bill Voorhees
Publicity: David Elzer/DEMAND PR

Characters:

Joy Ride: #88mph. Our protagonist. She's stoic, and strong, radiates power even though she's quiet. Can be a little bit of a dreamer. Late 20s, Black.

Michelle: Joy's girlfriend. Even tougher than Joy. Sometimes immature, extremely driven. Late 20s, White.

Lizzie Lightning: #100. The star of the team. Loud, cocky, funny, driven. Can be crude. Early 30s, Latinx.

Andrea the Vagiant: A former derby player, she's the coach of the Brooklyn Scallywags now. As large as her name, no-nonsense and loves the game. Mid-late 30s, Race neutral.

Anna-Stecia: #98.6. One of the older players, she's experienced and reliable, has a well spoken loud mouth. A nurse in her non-derby life. Late 30s, early 40s Black.

Hot Flash: #55. The oldest of the players. A mom, brass, funny, a real Brooklynite. Early 50s, White.

Squeaky Mouse: #5.0. One of the younger players. Is usually adorable without trying but still has a tough side to her. Early 20s, Race neutral.

Diaz de los Muertos: #1101. Tough talking, no nonsense, has a lot of heart and passion in everything she does. Best friends with Anna, mid-late 20s, Latina.

Prosecute-Her: #665. The other younger of the players, she's a genius and a law student. Early 20s, Asian.

*Any of these characters (with the exception of Hot Flash) may be cast with trans/non-binary actors.

Setting:

Usually in a locker room in Coney Island.
Sometimes in a bedroom in New Jersey.
And some places in between; a car, a tattoo shop, a dance club,
But everything takes place ontop of a roller derby track.

Time: 2015

Note: Women are not on skates at any point through the play; moments of skating are represented by dance. This is a Dance-ical. Dances move the story forward and invoke the movement of roller derby, when indicated.

Playwrights Note:

When sentences end without punctuation, there is something unfinished about them. The next sentence does not cut off the first but comes quickly after.

FOR THE LOVE OF (or, the roller derby play)

Prologue

(We hear the sounds of a game before the lights come up. Cheers and jeers from the crowd, shouts from the women, whistles from the refs, indicating violations.
The lights slowly come up, there's a group of women on a derby track. They're in the middle of a game. This dance movement looks like the closest to an actual game would sans skates.
As the lights slowly come up, so does music slowly begin to take over the sounds of the game until
It's full dance and
Full music.
LIZZIE breaks free of the pack. Everyone begins to move in slow motion and the crowd sounds like it's underwater. She watches them. Speaks to us.)

LIZZIE: It's called the pack.
　　All of us, together like that.
　　The point is for the Jammer? To get through the pack.
　　There's one on each team, a Jammer, we wear the stars on our helmets. And so the Jammer's gotta get through. Be the first one to get through.
　　That's the point.
　　To score the points.
　　She's gotta break through then go around and score points for each player she passes.

(She passes through the other players – none of them notice her. Her words match her action.)

And the other jammer, she's gotta get through the pack, too, you know. So it winds up being a chase.
Who can score the most points.
Who can pass the most players.
That's the point.

So…yeah, that's it, pretty much. I mean, there's a shit ton of rules and it can get complicated but for the most part, that's it.

It's a rush.

(JOY breaks out of the pack, dances solo while LIZZIE watches.)

We don't get shit for doing it – it actually costs a shit-ton of money to do it, skates and dues and gear and shit.

But you can't do anything but do it.

I can't do anything but do it.

The chase. It's all about the chase. Who can get through first, who can last the longest, who can catch the other.

That's what makes it exciting.

It's crazy how we get so caught up in it, you know? How it becomes everything.

I guess that's what makes it fun.

I guess that's what makes it something.

(LIZZIE joins in the dance.)

The getting caught up.

Getting caught up with the crowd and the wow. Forgetting how to breathe, heart pounding, heart thumping and bumping, getting caught up with the game.

The chase and the game.

(The sound of the crowd and the game swells and swells and swells until –)

Scene I

(A woman's locker room. Three women are there – HOT FLASH, ANNA-STECIA and PROSECUTE-HER. PROSE-CUTE-HER is in her full gear but sitting against the wall, her laptop plugged into an outlet. She's frantically typing away, like her life depends on it. ANNA and HOT are getting their gear on, doing some stretches and other warm-ups.)

PROSECUTE-HER: Quick, what's another word for challenges?

ANNA: Use the thesaurus

PROSECUTE-HER: Yeah, I already used all these words.

(HOT's phone begins to ring. It's something funky. She fumbles for her phone.)

ANNA: So make one up.

PROSECUTE-HER: I can't make one up

(HOT answers the phone.)

HOT FLASH: Yeah, Ronald, what?

PROSECUTE-HER: Just throw me a word

ANNA: Like what

HOT FLASH: Well he's gotta

PROSECUTE-HER: Like another word, like, like, like

ANNA: For challenges?

PROSECUTE-HER: Yeah, like, like, like

ANNA: difficulties?

9

(JOY enters. In the chaos, she goes unnoticed.)

HOT FLASH: Well I don't give a shit,

PROSECUTE-HER: No, that won't work

HOT FLASH: he's getting too old for this!

(SQUEAKY MOUSE enters, starts getting ready immediately.)

HOT FLASH: I don't got time, I ain't even got my top on.

ANNA: I dunno, hardships?

PROSECUTE-HER: No that won'-
Wait

(She goes back to typing frantically.)

ANNA: You're welcome

(ANDREA enters.)

ANDREA: Ten minutes, ladies! I don't wanna start any later
than 10:30, you all understand? I wanna scrape my sorry ass
outta here at 1am the laaaatest. Got it?

ALL: Yeah, yeah, etc

ANDREA: Anybody see Lizzie?

ANNA: Not here

ANDREA: 'Course not.
Tell her I'm looking for her.

(ANDREA leaves, DIAZ enters, on the phone.)

DIAZ: *(phone)* Well I don't give a shit, if I come home and
that shit's not washed I'm gonna kill you

HOT FLASH: *(phone)* All right, put him on.

DIAZ: *(phone)* Don't test me

PROSECUTE-HER: *(to no one)* What's another word for I'm fucked?

ANNA: *(to PH)* You still have like ten minutes

HOT FLASH: *(phone)* Hey baby, whatsamatter you don't wanna go to bed?

PROSECUTE-HER: *(to Anna)* No, I ONLY have ten minutes

DIAZ: *(phone)* No, no, yeah really, yes, I will!

PROSECUTE-HER: *(to Anna)* I can't even take a shit in ten minutes

ANNA: *(to PH)* Well, then, maybe you can't

DIAZ: *(phone)* Does it sound like I'm kidding?

PROSECUTE-HER: *(to herself)* Fuck.

DIAZ: *(phone)* because I'm not fucking kidding David, David, DAVID you're gonna make me have to count to ten

PROSECUTE-HER: *(to Diaz)* Hey, Diaz can you NOT? I can't fucking think

DIAZ: *(to PH)* Oh, I'm sorry, I didn't know this was a fucking library, I didn't realize we were in a study hall, I thought this was a locker room, I'm sorry, my mistake!
(to David) okay listen I gotta go I GOTTA GO BYE DAVID
Byeiloveyoubye

(She hangs up the phone.)

11

DIAZ: Asshole

ANNA: So how's David?

DIAZ: Fine

(They do a complicated handshake.)

DIAZ: Yo, you got a tweezer?

ANNA: Yeah, here

(Throws it.)

DIAZ: Thanks. I got this extra long boobie hair that's freakin' me out.

ANNA: Hate those.

MOUSE: Hey, how often do you guys shave your pits?

ANNA: Everyday

DIAZ: Yeah, same.

MOUSE: Yeah, I mean, it's like a beard, right, like I can shave it in the morning and then by 5:00 it's like all back? And like I don't even mind the hair, it feels like grass, kinda? But I start to stink. Like, rancid. Even with deodorant, no matter what I do.

PROSECUTE-HER: I need a word for-
Wait, no never mind.

HOT FLASH: Mommy loves you, okay? You believe me?

ANDREA: THREE MINUTES

HOT FLASH: Wattayamean No?

MOUSE: Like, I even tried plucking them out

ANNA: Plucking what out?

MOUSE: My armpit hairs

ANNA/DIAZ: WHAT/WHY?!

MOUSE: What, so that it gets like the root

HOT FLASH: *(still on the phone but talking to everyone)*
That's not how it works, honey, no

MOUSE: What, it's just like waxing

ANNA: So just wax them

MOUSE: Yeah but it's cool, you can see like the sweat drop-
lets on the roots

DIAZ: You're gross

PROESECUTE-HER: Wait, listen to this –
The difficulties I have faced have risen above me, like
mountains that rise from the ocean. But instead of allowing
them to stop me in my path, I have appreciated all of these
mountainous challenges because they have pushed me to the
point in my life where I am now. These hardships have
sharpened my experience so I can –
Wait, no wait that makes no sense.
This whole thing makes no sense.
Shit shit shit if I don't have this done then I'm gonna be
fuckin' fucked

MOUSE: Here, smell this –

(Shoves her equipment in JOY RIDE's face.)

JOY RIDE: Holy shit

MOUSE: Rancid, right?

ANNA: Man, just put your shit on, ain't nobody got time for your stank-ass stench.

MOUSE: I know, it smells really bad.

(She smells her gear.)

ANNA: You're Joy Ride, right?

JOY RIDE: Yeah.

DIAZ: Oh yeah, you're the rookie that wiped out during try outs.

JOY RIDE: Right.

DIAZ: That shit was hot.

(Does an impression of Joy wiping out at try outs.)

ANNA: Welcome to the team.
    You ready for tonight?

DIAZ: Obviously, she's madd early

JOY: Oh yeah, I just –

ANDREA: *(from off)* What the hell is going on in there, why is there nobody ON THE TRACK

DIAZ: We'll see you out there.

(ANNA and DIAZ skate out.)

HOT FLASH: I'll be back before you wake up. *(Makes a lot of kissy noises into the phone.)*

(PROSECUTE-HER slams her laptop shut.)

PROSECUTE-HER: Fuck it, I'm fucking fucked fuck

(She skates out.)

JOY RIDE: What's up with her?

SQUEAKY MOUSE: That's Prosecute-Her. She's a law student or something, I forget, so she's always stressed out. I'm Squeaky Mouse. I'm never stressed out. Sorry I shoved my shit in your face.

JOY RIDE: No, that's okay, it smelled…fine.

SQUEAKY MOUSE: I know, like hot *Cheetos*, right?

JOY RIDE: Oh, I don't really eat *Cheetos*

SQUEAKY MOUSE: They're the best snack food.
    Why are you here?

JOY RIDE: Because it's practice?

SQUEAKY MOUSE: Yeah but no I mean the new girls didn't have to get here until later

JOY RIDE: Yeah, I'm just –

SQUEAKY MOUSE: -an overachiever?

JOY RIDE: Guess so.

(HOT FLASH, hangs up, starts to put her shirt on, gets stuck.)

HOT FLASH: Fuck

SQUEAKY MOUSE: You okay, Hot Flash?

HOT FLASH: I'm fuckin' stuck and I'm gettin a flash, I'm fine.

(ANDREA enters.)

ANDREA: How long is three minutes to you?
Does that mean fifteen?
And where the FUCK is Lizzie?

SQUEAKY MOUSE: Not here yet.

ANDREA: It's ten fuckin' forty

HOT FLASH: No shit.

ANDREA: The new girls'll be here in 20 fuckin' minutes

SQUEAKY MOUSE: One's already here.

ANDREA: The fuck're you doing here so early?

JOY RIDE: I just... didn't have anywhere else to be?

ANDREA: That's sad

JOY RIDE: No, I mean, I live in Jersey –

HOT FLASH: Fuckin' Jersey?

JOY RIDE: Yeah, so –

HOT FLASH: The fuck you're coming out to Brooklyn for?
Jersey's got teams.

JOY RIDE: Yeah, but I got on the Brooklyn Scallywags
so...I'm here.

ANDREA: And we're the best.

JOY RIDE: Damn right.

HOT FLASH: The trains are a hot mess at night.

JOY RIDE: I don't know, I mean, I drive so -

SQUEAKY MOUSE: You drove?

JOY RIDE: Well, yeah

SQUEAKY MOUSE: I still don't know how to drive

JOY RIDE: I mean, I never used to when I lived in Brooklyn. Kind of need a car in Jersey

SQUEAKY: I mean, I do and don't wish I could drive. I don't because it's like stupid to drive around during the day with all the traffic but I do because the trains are stupid at night. You know?

JOY: Sure

SQUEAKY: Right

JOY: I mean would – would you want a ride? Home?

SQUEAKY: For real?

HOT FLASH: I do

JOY: Sure, why not?

SQUEAKY: That would be awesome

(LIZZIE LIGHTNING enters. She's like lightning, electrifying the room.)

MOUSE: Shit

HOT FLASH: We'll talk after practice.

(HOT and MOUSE leaves. JOY awkwardly stands.)

ANDREA: The fuck, Lizzie-

17

LIZZIE: I know

ANDREA: We were supposed-

LIZZIE: I know, you don't gotta start, the fuckin' trains don't run this late.

ANDREA: So what're you gonna do about it.

LIZZIE: Put my shit on and practice.

ANDREA: Every week?

LIZZIE: I'll figure it out.

ANDREA: You better
You're captain, you gotta-

LIZZIE: Yo, I know.

ANDREA: It's a team

LIZZIE: Jesus Christ, is it?

ANDREA: We'll talk about this later.

LIZZIE: Yeah, lucky me. I'm sure we will.

(She leaves. LIZZIE puts her stuff on at lightning speed.)

LIZZIE: Who're you?

JOY RIDE: New.

LIZZIE: That your name?

JOY RIDE: Joy. Joy Ride.

LIZZIE: Joy Joy Ride?

JOY RIDE: No, just Joy Ride.

LIZZIE: That's cool.

JOY RIDE: Yeah.
My name's really Joy. That's my real name. I just added the ride.

LIZZIE: Clever.

JOY RIDE: Thanks.

LIZZIE: I'm Lizzie Lightning.

JOY RIDE: I know.

LIZZIE: Yeah?

JOY RIDE: Yeah I mean, who doesn't?

LIZZIE: I like you.

JOY RIDE: Thanks.

LIZZIE: Sorry you had to see that. Andrea's a huge pain in my ass.
I mean, I live in fuckin' East New York, right, and it takes me over an hour to get here on a good day but trains don't run at night, like at all, I mean, they do but not as frequent, so I gotta leave my place at like 8 to get here by 10:30 but fuckin' I couldn't today, I had a client that wouldn't stop shaking – I do tattoos, I'm an artist – and this poor mother-fucker, big dude, he could not get his shit together and I was doin' a big one on his calf and I had to go like centimeter by centimeter because he just kept shaking like spazzing out. I finally had to give him like three shots of Jack to get him to calm down and then he got TOO calm and turned into a limp fuckin' rag so it was just a mess and by the time I get the outline done, bam, it's 8:30 and he's crying which is all my fault between the ink and the whiskey so I gotta calm him

down and close up the shop, so what'm I supposed to do about it? Fly here? Practice'll start whether or not I'm here, it don't matter, shit.

JOY: You know, I have a car

LIZZIE: So what

JOY: So I could drive you home.

LIZZIE: Nah
Yeah?

JOY: Yeah. I mean, I already offered it to some of the others. Better steal a spot before they're all gone.

LIZZIE: Your name suits you.
Joy Ride.

JOY: Yours does, too.

LIZZIE: See you out there.

JOY: Sure.

(LIZZIE zips out.
Sound of skates and warm up melts into -)

Scene II

(MICHELLE and JOY's bedroom.
MICHELLE sits on the bed cross legged, a sketchpad in her lap.
She's on the phone – on a headset so her hands are free to sketch.)

MICHELLE: Yes. Yes. No, yes, I understand, I completely understand Ms. Buckley, the shade of green does look like puke. It does. Yes, it does. I agree. I'm agreeing with you. The color was saturated – yes, okay.

*(JOY enters. MICHELLE waves, blows a kiss, turns the pad around, there's a sketch on it, something like **Make it stop!** Or something, you know, better than that, that conveys her disgust at the situation.*
They play around while MICHELLE attempts to complete the phone call.)

MICHELLE: Sure, Ms. Buckley, we'll fix it, no charge, no problem.
No, no problem, I'm here to help. Happy to help. Ok, now, Ms. Buckley, good night, good night, now.

(She drops the phone like she's dropping the miccc yeahhh handled that shit!)

JOY: What was all that about?

MICHELLE: Work emergency

JOY: It's after midnight

MICHELLE: Well, her husband thought the green on the shower curtain looked like puke.
It was "Puke colored"

JOY: That doesn't make any sense, puke can be an assortment of colors.

MICHELLE: I know, right? My puke's always yellow

JOY: Mine's pink

MICHELLE: but her husband was adamant and when you're the VP of Sarah's Shower Curtains you just have to work until the job is done.

JOY: Wait, what?
VP?!
Does that stand for what I think it stands for?

MICHELLE: Violin Princess

JOY: Vice President?!

MICHELLE: Yes!

JOY: Yes?!

MICHELLE: Yes!

(JOY whoops and they celebrate together, maybe do a dance, it's really, realllly fun.)

JOY: When the fuck did that happened?!

MICHELLE: I mean, they offered it to me a few weeks ago but we were in negotiations for a few weeks so I didn't want to say anything until it was officially official and today, it was, it is, you may call me Missus Vice President

JOY: Babe, that's crazy, that's great
So you'll be designing more?

MICHELLE: Oh, no

JOY: No?

MICHELLE: I'll actually probably be designing a little less –

JOY: What?

MICHELLE: -which is fine, it's not forever.
It's fine.

JOY: Michelle.

MICHELLE: And, I mean, the work's interesting

JOY: But you hate it

MICHELLE: I don't *hate* it

JOY: That's not what -

MICHELLE: So?
Are you going to tell me how it went?

JOY: Michelle –

MICHELLE: How'd it go?
Were you a superstar?

JOY: Don't you want to -

MICHELLE: Were they like oh shit, who's that girl

JOY: I don't really want to talk about that –

MICHELLE: Were they like "This girl was born with skates
instead of feet -"

JOY: No, no they weren't, they weren't any of that.
I was awful.

MICHELLE: I'm sure it wasn't that bad

JOY: You're right, it wasn't.
It was worse.

MICHELLE: Joy –

JOY: Basic. I was basically Basic.

MICHELLE: You're not Basic.

JOY: Yeah well tonight I was.

MICHELLE: You're like the most un-basic bitch there is.

JOY: Nah.

MICHELLE: Like, ever.

JOY: Stop

MICHELLE: Like in the history of all things, ever, you, Joy, are the least basic person there ever was or will be.

JOY: You're just sayin' that because you like me.

MICHELLE: You're just new. Things are hard when they're new.

JOY: That's like some Sesame Street shit you just pulled out right there

MICHELLE: Will you stop, I'm trying to be inspirational –

JOY: All right, some Mister Rogers shit -

MICHELLE: Why are you hating on my inspiration?

JOY: I just thought I was better than this.

MICHELLE: I already think you're great

(She kisses JOY.
The two start to get ready for bed during the following.)

JOY: Maybe I should quit

MICHELLE: What, after one practice?

JOY: Yes.

MICHELLE: You're not serious

JOY: You weren't there

MICHELLE: You can't just quit, Joy. You've been talking about doing this for a year, you can't just quit because one practice – your first practice - was shitty. You'll get better. You know why? Because. Practice makes perfect.

JOY: My God, you're really unstoppable tonight

MICHELLE: I'm just happy! I'm really happy. Happy that I got my promotion, happy you got your derby practice, happy. It's a nice night to be happy. Right?

(They're in bed. MICHELLE reaches over for JOY. Takes her hand and kisses it.)

JOY: Thanks.

MICHELLE: Yeah.

JOY: Mrs. Rogers.

MICHELLE: I'll take it.

(Pause.)

JOY: Oh, so you know who's on the team?

MICHELLE: Who?

JOY: Lizzie Lightning

MICHELLE: Who's that?

JOY: The star

MICHELLE: Of what?

JOY: No one, never mind

MICHELLE: No, who is she?

JOY: Just like… the best player in the league.
    Kind of in the world.

MICHELLE: You mean next to you?

JOY: Michelle

MICHELLE: What?

JOY: I'm being serious.

MICHELLE: Me, too!

JOY: Okay.

(Pause. JOY turns off the light.)

MICHELLE: Are you going to tell me who she is?

JOY: I just did, she's the best player in the league.

MICHELLE: Okay.

(Pause.)

JOY: That's really it.

MICHELLE: Okay.

(Silence.)

JOY: She's really different, though.

MICHELLE: Who?

JOY: Lizzie Lightning.

MICHELLE: Can't you call her just Lizzie?

JOY: I guess. I dunno. I mean, she wasn't even supposed to be on the team, it was a last minute switch and boom, there she is, team captain. It's kindafa mindfuck. Watching her sweat up close and realizing she's not a goddess of the track, she's actually just...a person. Her skin's made of skin, not metal. And hearing her talk. That's weird, too. It's kindaf the weirdest, actually. I never realized I didn't know how she sounded until I heard her talk. But she talks just like she jams, all tough, barreling over sentences she don't got time to hear, and she's like mean and strong and she both is and isn't Lizzie Lightning, all at the same time.
Does that make any sense?
Michelle?
Miche?
Babe.

(MICHELLE is sleeping.
JOY tries not to let the disappointment burn her skin.
She gets out of bed, walks to the fire escape. She sits there and the sound of a crowd is heard before the voice of an announcer announces:)

ANNOUNCER: Introducing the two-thousand-fifteen team, reigning champs for the fifth year running, the one and only Brooklyn Scallywags!
NoOOOooow presenting number 98.6, she'll knock you out, put your hands together for ANNA-STECIA

(ANNA walks on, holding a clipboard and wearing scrubs. The sounds stop suddenly. She walks over to a patient, checks her chart. Notices that she's awake.)

ANNA-STECIA: Hey Mrs. Jonson, what are you doing awake? It's too late for that.
Or too early. *(What time is it?)* It's just after midnight. You should really be sleeping.
(The damn moon's keeping me up)   Well, I can close the shade if you want. I'm surprised the moon is so bright tonight. Almost like the sun.
I wish I could crawl right in that bed with you and go to sleep, these night shifts are killing me. I'm getting too old for this shit. Who says that? From the movie? I'm getting too old for this shit! Well, it's true, whoever said it.
Anyway, let's see what we have here – oh shit! Mrs. Jonson! You pooped today? Why didn't you tell me, hell yeah, give me a high five, right here, that's awesome! That means you can go home. *(I know, they told me)*   So you better get some sleep, can't be going home tired.
You want me to get you another pillow? *(No)*   You want me to get you anything? *(No).*   All right then, you just holler if you need me.
(Turns to leave. Stops and turns back.)
Just tell me one thing.
Did you look? After you pooped?
(Don't be gross!)
I mean, I'm just saying, I would've
All right, Mrs. Jonson, bye.
(Wait)
Yes?
(Call me Eleanor)
All right Eleanor. You take care of yourself.
You take care.

(She walks away from the moment, into the derby world. The rest of the team crowd around her, all of them skating in place until they begin to circle, circle all around until they're all together, all circling together and it moves into –)

28

Scene III

(JOY's car. HOT FLASH sits in the front. DIAZ and LIZZIE in the back.)

HOT FLASH: So the other day I come home from work to a completely silent house, it's like si-lent and I go into the living room and there's Ronnie, sitting on the couch with his laptop in his lap, playing that damn online poker shit and I'm like Babe! And he's like Yeah and I'm like Where's the kid?
I dunno
Wattaya mean YOU don't know, you were watching him
Kid's in the bathroom, crayon all smashed in the floor. Ronnie could give a crap, barely batted an eye "I like how it looks" he goes OH I could just strangle him.

DIAZ: Yes, you know what, yes, I could strangle David sometimes. I swear, ever since we moved in, he hasn't stopped talking and it's just like sometimes I need my own space, right, but he don't leave me alone, I swear he'd follow me into the bathroom if he could.
Does that feeling ever go away?

HOT FLASH: Sometimes. Depends on the man

LIZZIE: or woman

HOT FLASH: Yeah yeah, it just depends. Ronnie's my second and it's not that he's better than the first, he just fights alongside me instead of just with me.
Feel me?

JOY: Damn.

DIAZ: Yo, that was deep

HOT FLASH: Not really

DIAZ: What about you, Joy?

29

HOT FLASH: Yeah, got any headaches?

JOY: Me? No.

LIZZIE: Single?

JOY: No. Just… no headaches.
  Michelle is great.

LIZZIE: Cute

HOT FLASH: How long you been together?

JOY: A while.

LIZZIE: Yeah?

JOY: Yeah.

(HOT FLASH'S phone rings.)

DIAZ: That's cool.

HOT FLASH: Hello?

DIAZ: Are you like gonna get married and shit?

HOT FLASH: Yeah, yeah, I'm coming!

DIAZ: You can do that now, you know

HOT FLASH: When are we gonna –

JOY: Here, I'm pulling over-

HOT FLASH: SHE'S PULLIN – you know what, I'm hanging
  up HANGING UP k love you, too.
  Thanks so much for the ride, Joy. You rock.

(She gets out.)

DIAZ: You know what, I think imma get out here, too.

JOY: Sure?

DIAZ: Yeah. I wanna walk.

LIZZIE: That smart?

DIAZ: Just wanna get some air.
Not ready to go home yet.

JOY: All right.
I hope you feel better about David

DIAZ: Ah, what can you do?
I love the jerk.
Thanks for the ride, chica.

JOY: No problem.

LIZZIE: See ya.

*(She gets out. JOY waves to her and puts the car into motion.
LIZZIE climbs into the front seat.)*

JOY: Hey, what, what are you doing?

LIZZIE: Moving.

JOY: Yeah, you coulda used the door!

LIZZIE: Where's the fun in that?

JOY: You're crazy.

LIZZIE: I'm efficient.

(She drives in silence for a moment.)

LIZZIE: So.
How'd you meet?

JOY: Who, Diaz?

LIZZIE: No. Your girl.

JOY: Oh, right. Duh.
Uh, college.
Wow, college.

LIZZIE: What's so wow about it?

JOY: Just – been a while, college was like almost ten years ago.
Shit.
She was this total anarchist artist, used to do the craziest shit. Like, once she broke a thousand eggs – literally, a thousand eggs – and glued the shells to this wall, in between the cracks of the wall, and somehow made it so all these flowers were growing out of the eggs that were in the cracks of this wall – it was crazy. She saved all the yolks, we had a lot of omelets.
But yeah, she was pretty cool. She's pretty cool.

(She stops the car.)

JOY: We're here.

(LIZZIE gets out of the car, climbs up on the hood.)

JOY: What are you doing?!

LIZZIE: Come on

JOY: Get your ass off my car!

LIZZIE: Let's look at the stars.

JOY: Seriously, it's smudging the glass

LIZZIE: I'll clean it, just come, look at the stars with me.

JOY: There's no stars.

LIZZIE: Pretend

(JOY gets out of the car. LIZZIE points at the sky.)

LIZZIE: Look, see?

JOY: Yeah, looks like a black sky.

LIZZIE: Come here

(JOY sits at the edge of the hood but doesn't lie down.)

LIZZIE: See, look.
There's the little dipper.
And the Big Dipper.
And Ryan's belt

JOY: Orion's.

LIZZIE: That's what I said.

JOY: Sure.

(JOY stares at the sky.)

JOY: You can see the stars out where I'm at in Jersey. But I
like this better.

LIZZIE: Yeah?

JOY: Yeah.
This is how I saw the sky growing up.
A dark endless sky. Looks like home.

LIZZIE: I didn't know you're from Brooklyn

JOY: Flatbush

LIZZIE: Bushwick
Before the hipsters priced me out.

JOY: Yeah, me too.

(Beat. It's nice to find someone from Brooklyn.)

LIZZIE: Yeah, why else would you be in Jersey?

JOY: Right?
Fucking sucks.
Michelle got a job out there so we had to move.

LIZZIE: What, she couldn't commute?

JOY: It made more sense
or something.

(They stare at the sky. JOY leans back a little bit more.)

JOY: I used to run.

LIZZIE: From what?

JOY: No, I mean, in college –

LIZZIE: I know what you meant

JOY: Oh

LIZZIE: I mean, I figured.
I don't mean to make you nervous.

JOY: You don't.

LIZZIE: Okay.

JOY: I'm not, I'm just tired.

LIZZIE: I should *(let you go)*

JOY: I was supposed to be in the Olympics.

LIZZIE: Get out.

JOY: Yeah, that's what I went to college for, I was there on a scholarship. I was good. Fast. And then I wasn't fast enough. I kept losing time. No matter what I did, milliseconds then seconds began to stick to my time, no matter how fast I went. I dreamt of running, I dreamt my feet were wings instead of feet and I'd wake up and run and they'd be concrete instead.

LIZZIE: Well. That sucks.

JOY: Yeah. It did.

(Silence but for city sounds.)

JOY: It's different.
  Derby.
  Better.

LIZZIE: Yeah?

JOY: Different.
  You're by yourself but
  you're not.
  I like that.
  It's nice to not be alone.

LIZZIE: You're good, you know.

JOY: Nah

LIZZIE: Getting good. You got good instincts out there. You don't freeze up. You might be fearless.
  We should work together. Out there on the track.

JOY: How?

LIZZIE: We can come up with some strategies. I can teach you.
I think we can be a good team.
Don't you?

JOY: Maybe.

LIZZIE: Think about it.

(LIZZIE stands, staring at the sky.)

LIZZIE: It's nice, isn't it? When the City is this quiet this late. Feels like it's endless. Then the daytime comes and it's not there no more. Where does it go?

JOY: I don't know.

LIZZIE: Good night, Joy Ride.
See you another time.

(She leaves. JOY sits on the hood of her car for a little longer. The sound of the crowd again, an announcer announces.)

ANNOUNCER: Ladies and gentlemen, put your hands together for number 55, HOT FLASH!

(She enters carrying a basket of laundry. She folds socks while she speaks.)

HOT FLASH: Yo, Ronnie! You'll never guess what Linda just told me – Linda, Linda – yeah, Lazy Eye Linda from the choir, right, so you know Linda, she's around our age and her and her husband aren't together no more – I forget, I think he cheated on her – I know, right, whoever did it's gotta be pretty desperate, it's not like he's got money – anyway, she's on one of those dating sites, for the old people, and she's gonna meet this guy for coffee, at the Starbucks. So she goes, she's waiting and he don't show up, so she leaves, all pissed off, and picks up her daughter for the airport and her daughter's like Oh what a stiff, forget him, right, so she does. Meanwhile, fast forward to today, guess who's in the obituary?

Her fucking date!

Can you get a load of that?

I guess he really was a stiff.

Hey Ronnie?

You still Like me? Yeah? Even after all these years? And the Kid?

Yeah, I guess I still Like you, too.

Are you gonna help me put this shit away or what?

(Lights shift and HOT FLASH walks off as we enter -)

Scene IV

(JOY and MICHELLE's bedroom. A different night.)

JOY: Get a load of this

(She flexes and her muscles be poppin'.)

JOY: You see these guns?

MICHELLE: I ain't blind

JOY: You see these guns?

MICHELLE: Heyyy nowww

JOY: You see these

(They start doing a silly dance together, set to the general chorus of "you see these guns" which is just rhythmic and silly. MICHELLE grabs her and starts kissing her.)

JOY: Am I about to get lucky?

MICHELLE: You mean you don't feel lucky every day when you wake up beside my beautiful smiling face?

JOY: You're such a tease.

(They kiss more. It gets passionate. MICHELLE takes off JOY's shirt and sees that she has a huge dark bruise on her stomach.)

MICHELLE: Holy shit.

JOY: Will you look at that.

MICHELLE: That looks horrible!

JOY: Battle wound.

(She tries to kiss MICHELLE again but MICHELLE is distracted by the bruise.)

JOY: Baby?
 Come on, it's fine.

MICHELLE: It's awful.

JOY: What did you expect? That I'd be untouchable?

MICHELLE: No, it's just -

JOY: Did you think just because I'm black that I can't get black and blues? Because honey, that's racist

MICHELLE: Shut up

(She playfully pushes her and JOY grabs her and holds her. They look at one another. MICHELLE kisses her fully.)

MICHELLE: Damn. It didn't work.

JOY: What?

MICHELLE: I tried to heal you with my kiss.

JOY: Baby, that only works for straight people.

MICHELLE: My bad.

JOY: We gonna do this or what?

MICHELLE: Hell yeah

(They try getting into it again but MICHELLE is being extra careful.)

JOY: Babe, what are you doing, what is this

MICHELLE: I just
 don't want to hurt you

JOY: Come on Michelle, you're not hurting me.

MICHELLE: Do you have any other bruises I don't know about?

JOY: Babe, I didn't even know about this one, seriously.
My whole body is just one giant constant ache
but I know what'll make me feel better –

(Reaches for MICHELLE – she's still hesitant.)

JOY: Michelle, come on. It's a sport, it's a contact sport, sports cause bruises.

MICHELLE: Yeah but still – I just didn't realize
Can I see it again?

(MICHELLE bends down and gently kisses JOY's bruise.)

JOY: It's a miracle! I'm healed!

MICHELLE: Shut up

JOY: I mean, we're on skates, it would be harder to not get a bruise than to get a bruise.

MICHELLE: You still like it?

JOY: Oh yeah, I love it.
I can't wait for the first game.
You're coming right?

MICHELLE: Of course, wouldn't want to miss my girlfriend getting pummeled

JOY: Oh, stop, it

MICHELLE: Of course I'm gonna go see your game, I'm proud of you.
Even if you beat yourself up.

And get home after midnight.
And we never see each other anymore.

JOY: Don't be so dramatic

MICHELLE: Who's being dramatic?

(MICHELLE does something dramatic.
JOY dramatically responds.
They're being silly together, both on the bed together, looking
at one another.
After a moment.)

JOY: I was actually thinking – now that you got your promotion and everything, maybe we could move back to Brooklyn.

MICHELLE: But I work in Jersey

JOY: But we got the car, you could drive in

MICHELLE: Everyday?

JOY: That's what I'm doing

MICHELLE: Yeah, but that's different, your schedule's more
flexible

JOY: But then derby goes so late

MICHELLE: Yeah but that's only 3 nights a week so

JOY: We'll probably see each other more.
Don't you miss Brooklyn?

MICHELLE: It's too expensive.

JOY: There are still spots that aren't

MICHELLE: Come on, you don't want to talk about this now

JOY: Then when are we going to talk about it?

MICHELLE: Let's talk about it later

JOY: So you'll think about it.

MICHELLE: Right.
We'll both think about it.
Okay?
Now, come on.
Let me explore you for bruises.

(They begin kissing again. It gets passionate.

The women begin to circle around the bed. It becomes a training montage.
They're doing drills – both on and off skates.
As it progresses, it turns into more of a dance until -)

Scene V

(The end of practice.
All of the ladies are getting back into street clothes.)

ANNA: My fuckin' back

HOT FLASH: I'm definitely too old for this shit

DIAZ: Then why'd you hit me so hard?

HOT FLASH: Adrenaline

PROSECUTE-HER: That'd be a great derby name

LIZZIE LIGHTNING: For sure

PROSECUTE-HER: Ann-dreneline

LIZZIE: How you holding up, rookie?

JOY RIDE: Great.

LIZZIE: Sure.

(She grabs her shoulders and begins to give her a massage.)

JOY: *(Moans)* That hurts

LIZZIE: Yeah?

JOY: Don't stop

SQUEAKY MOUSE: Guys, look at this one

(Shows off a bruise.)

SQUEAKY MOUSE: That's gonna look awesome tomorrow

DIAZ: That's nothing, I got one in the shape of Jay Leno on my ass

ANNA: Who's that?

DIAZ: You know

HOT FLASH: The guy with the chin

LIZZIE: You like?

ANNA: Oh yeah

JOY RIDE: Oh Yeah

(The sound of a phone ringing can be heard. ANDREA enters, but nobody really pays attention.)

ANDREA: Ladies
    Ladies.
    LADIES!
    Don't tell me I have to do the clapping thing, the clapping thing like we're in kindergarten

(Does the clapping thing, they start to pay attention until they're quiet.)

ANDREA: All right ladies, good practice, thanks. I'm seeing some hustle out there, some tight defense – remember, they can't score the points if they can't get past us. Right?
    Right.
    We got this.
    What do we know about Manhattan?

DIAZ: They got sloppy uniforms

ANDREA: I'm serious –

DIAZ: So'm I, you seen them? They raggedy.

ANDREA: All right, besides their alleged poor taste in uniform, what do we know?

(Sound of a phone ringing.)

MOUSE: They suck

ANDREA: Their defense –

LIZZIE: Don't do shit

ANDREA: Their defense is tight.

DIAZ: I guess

PROSECUTE-HER: We're tighter

MOUSE: Yeah!

(They high five one another. The sound of a phone ringing.)

ANDREA: Yes, our defense is tight but that doesn't mean –

HOT FLASH: Has anyone seen my keys? I think they fell outta my bag

ANDREA: That doesn't mean –

PROSECUTE-HER: Where'd you see them last?

HOT FLASH: That is the most useless question

ANNA: Are we going to be much longer?

HOT FLASH: If I remembered where they was I wouldn't be lookin' for them!

(The sound of a phone ringing. ANDREA does the clapping thing again.)

ANDREA: HeyheyheyHEYHEY
   HEY.

(They all quiet down.)

MOUSE: Here they are!

ANDREA: Seriously?

MOUSE: Sorry.

ANDREA: I'm trying to talk to youse –

(The sound of a phone.)

ANDREA: Who's fucking phone is that?!

JOY: It's… I'm sorry, it's mine

ANDREA: You wanna answer it?

JOY: No, no, sorry

ANDREA: I dunno, it might be a real huge emergency –

JOY: No, it's fine.
   I put it on silent, it's fine.
   Sorry.

ANDREA: Fine.
   So we –

(The sound of a phone on vibrate.)

JOY: Shit

ANDREA: Go answer your fuckin' phone, Joy!

JOY: No, I'm sorry, it's fine –

ANDREA: Vibrate is not silent!
I fucking hate that noise like fuckin' buzzing

JOY: No, I'm sorry, it's off now, see? I'm turning it off.
I'm listening.

ANDREA: You sure nobody else has a comment to make before I continue? Everybody got their listening caps on?
Good. Imma make this quick so we can get out of here by
Sunday.
Squeaky Mouse, don't forget to stay low.
Anna,

ANNA: Yeah, I know, my elbows

ANDREA: Yeah, your elbows, keep 'em tucked, you don't
want them calling any bullshit out on you

ANNA: I can't help if they slip!

ANDREA: Which is why you need to keep them tucked.

PROSECUTE-HER: Ref's calls are crap half the time, it's as
though they're out to get us.

ANDREA: We're lucky that we have such dedicated Refs

LIZZIE: That're always powertripping.

ANDREA: Give it a rest, Lizzie.

LIZIE: You on their side?

ANDREA: I'm not saying they're right –

LIZZIE: What are you saying?

ANDREA: Here are the facts. We're facing Manhattan Outlaws in a week. A WEEK. We only got three more practices. That's nothing! It's nothing. We're a tight team but

47

we need to be tighter. We're gonna go head to head with them whether we're ready or not. I just want youse to be ready. That's all. All right?

(DIAZ lets out a huge, authentic but really obnoxious yawn. The ladies giggle.)

DIAZ: Sorry.

(They laugh harder. ANDREA does not.)

ANDREA: See you ladies tomorrow. Have a good night.

(ANDREA leaves. ANNA playfully hits DIAZ.)

ANNA: What'd you do that for?

DIAZ: What, I'm tired!
It's fuckin' authentic

ANNA: You crazy

PROSECUTE-HER: God, it's so fuckin' late and I still have to read like 300 pages by 8am

MOUSE: Who takes a class at 8am?

PROSECUTE-HER: I know, it sucks. At least the trains're running local, plenty of time to read.

HOT FLASH: That's optimistic

PROSECUTE-HER: Just call me Optimism Prime.

(She leaves.)

HOT FLASH: You ready, Joy?

JOY: I'll meet you guys at the car.

(DIAZ, SQUEAKY MOUSE and HOT FLASH leave. All the other ladies have left; it's just JOY and LIZZIE.)

LIZZIE: You all right?

JOY: Yeah, I just can't get my phone to turn back on. Piece of crap.

LIZZIE: Who was trying to call you?

JOY: I don't know.

LIZZIE: Could've answered

JOY: It's fine. I'm sure.
You okay?

LIZZIE: Sure.
Drea just doesn't know what she's talking about half the time. I'm sure you've realized by now.

JOY: She's all right.

LIZZIE: Dunno how we'll win that first game. Team's a mess.

JOY: That's not true –

LIZZIE: The other rookies aren't like you; they don't know what the fuck is going on. Brutal Noodle keeps clenching and who the hell knows what's going on in Lil' Hellman's peanut brain, half the time it's like she doesn't even know we're in the middle of a game.

JOY: Sounds like you should be the coach.

LIZZIE: Shut up.
Yeah?

JOY: Yeah.

LIZZIE: I just notice shit, that's all.

JOY: That's like one half of what a coach is supposed to do.

LIZZIE: Guess so.

JOY: Come on. I wanna get home.

(LIZZIE goes over to her and starts adjusting her shoulder.)

JOY: What're you doing?

LIZZIE: You feel that?

JOY: Sure?

LIZZIE: Your back? Makin' that line?

JOY: Mmm

LIZZIE: Keep that on the turns. You'll glide quicker.

(LIZZIE keeps her hand there a little longer.)

JOY: Thanks.

LIZZIE: No problem.

(She lets go quickly, gathers her things.)

LIZZIE: You ready or what?

(She leaves. JOY stands in the middle of the empty room. Feels where LIZZIE had just touched her. Smiles.)

Scene VI

(JOY and MICHELLE's bedroom. MICHELLE is sitting cross-legged on the bed, fully clothed, in the dark. She's holding her cell phone, staring at it like it's a mirror. JOY enters, trying to be quiet.)

MICHELLE: Where were you?

JOY: Jesus

MICHELLE: I called you like 20 times

JOY: What are you doing, sitting in the dark?

(She turns a light on.)

JOY: And awake.

MICHELLE: You didn't pick up

JOY: Yeah, I know, I'm sorry, coach made me turn it off and now, get this, it won't turn back on.

MICHELLE: Oh

JOY: Yeah, I know. Piece of crap. Look, look at this, it doesn't even flicker. I was trying it the whole way home –

MICHELLE: Can you put it down –

JOY: Oh, oh wait, look! It's turning on, it's actually turning on

MICHELLE: I need to tell you something

JOY: Thank god

MICHELLE: Joy

JOY: That would've sucked

MICHELLE: All right, well, I lost my fucking job.

(Beat.)

JOY: No.

MICHELLE: Yeah

JOY: How?

MICHELLE: I don't know

JOY: What does that mean?

MICHELLE: I mean, I just, I don't know

JOY: But you just got a promotion, they can't just fire you

MICHELLE: Except they can

JOY: We can fight this, right? It's obviously…it's not right, we're gonna fight this, it's bullshit

MICHELLE: No, it's-

JOY: Fuck them, we're gonna sue them, all right, we're gonna sue them and -

MICHELLE: I actually, I did something stupid? I mean, I did something.
I uh…took a risk. On a design. After my supervisor said not to, but I thought, if she could just see what I was trying to do - I didn't know she could fire me over it but she could. She did. Because I wasted company time and resources and it shows that I'm a liability.
I'm a fucking liability.
But I was just trying something that's never been tried before, that's all, that's all I was doing. I mean, it's just shower curtains.
It sucks.

(JOY takes her and hugs her and holds her.)

MICHELLE: I don't, I don't want this to be happening. I don't want it, I don't want it.

JOY: It's okay.

MICHELLE: What are we going to do?

JOY: We're gonna figure it out.
We will.

MICHELLE: How?

JOY: I'll pick up more shifts at the Foot Locker. They like me, they'll give them to me.
And you can do what you gotta do, we'll figure it out.

MICHELLE: This is impossible

JOY: It's not, we're gonna figure it out.
Okay? Do you believe me?

MICHELLE: Why didn't you pick up the phone?

JOY: I'm sorry

MICHELLE: You should've answered

JOY: I know –

MICHELLE: You should've answered
You should've answered.

JOY: I'm here now.
I'm here.
I'm not going anywhere.

MICHELLE: I lost my job

JOY: I know.

MICHELLE: I didn't mean to.

JOY: I know.
I know.

(JOY cradles MICHELLE as the lights shift into-)

Scene VII

(The same announcer from before.)

ANNOUNCER: Number 665, she'll throw the book at you, it's
Prosecute-Her!

*(PROSECUTE-HER sits alone with a giant book. She's trying
to memorize something insidious.)*

PROSECUTE-HER: In the case of Miller vs. Miller, the court
ruled in favor of the secondary party which meant –
Shit.
Shit!
How the fuck am I supposed to memorize all this bullshit?!
(Slams the book shut. Opens it again.)
In the case of Miller vs. Miller –
Fuck.
*(The sound of the crowd begins to creep into her brain. She
shakes her head to try to loosen it and it stops.)*
All right so
the point is to remember – remember the rules of the game
I mean, case,
just
*(The sound of the crowd again, louder this time, more persis-
tent. She speaks loudly over it.)*
It is often suggested to use mnemonic devices in order to
memorize useless facts and stuff your brain with pointless
knowledge
(The crowd mixed with the sound of skates. She stands up.)
Oh, fuck it

*(She starts to do a dance – a solo tap dance, tap dancing all
over the place, the sound of the game her background.
The other women come out and join her – her outfit turns into a
derby uniform.
The sound of the crowd swells and swells and the girls line up,
facing the audience, one by one. They form the pack. LIZZIE
skates in back of the pack – she's wearing a star on her helmet.
The sounds swell and swell and we hear.)*

ANNOUNCER: Ladies and gentlemen, boys and girls, children of all ages, are you ready for some Roller Derby? I said are you ready for some RoLLLER derby?! On the start of my whistle, Manhattan Outlaws vs. Brooklyn Scallywags, first game of the season about to take place, help me count it down now, we'll be starting in 5, 4, 3, 2, and

(The sound of a whistle. Blackout.)

Scene VIII

(The locker room at the end of the game.)

MOUSE: HOLY SHIT

ANNA: That was UNBELIEVABLE

JOY: Can you believe that shit?!

LIZZIE: What, you were worried?

JOY: Pfft, no

HOT FLASH: Yes

DIAZ: The last five minutes –

PROSECUTE-HER: Game of the century!

MOUSE: It's never been this close

DIAZ: Game of the year!

ANNA: Nuts

PROSECUTE-HER: Insane

JOY: Awesome

LIZZIE: You're welcome.

(ANDREA enters. The ladies greet her with cheers and screams of congratulations. ANDREA speaks above the noise.)

ANDREA: Well I hope you're all very proud of yourselves.

LIZZIE: Fuck yes

ANDREA: Won your first game of the season. First game of some of all your careers. First game.

(They all cheer some more. ANDREA starts doing an obnoxious slow clap.)

ANDREA: Congratulations.
You all skinned by by the seat of your pants.

(There's silence except for her slow clap which is obviously mocking.)

MOUSE: But

ANDREA: What? Am I wrong?
This was Luck.
Pure luck that this team won.
You know what, I don't even want to call it a team right now.

LIZZIE: Way to bring it down.

ANDREA: Nobody listened to me.

LIZZIE: Way to inspire your girls

ANDREA: Especially you. Especially you, Lizzie, you didn't listen to a single thing I said the second half.

LIZZIE: And it's a fuckin' good thing I didn't! You wanted me to play conservative, telling me to call off jams early–

ANDREA: You don't have to tell me, I was there

LIZZIE: So what if the other team scores a point if I could scoop up three more?

ANDREA: You were playing reckless

LIZZIE: We wouldn't've won!

JOY: Lizzie's kinda right

PROSECUTE-HER: Yeah, we were gonna lose

58

ANDREA: You're not in the position to say anything either, Lucy, six penalties in fifteen minutes?

PROSECUTE-HER: That's an exaggeration

ANDREA: You almost fouled out of the game!

PROSECUTE-HER: They kept making me skate back!

JOY: Yeah, Refs shoulda called it

PROSECUTE-HER: And they didn't

ANDREA: I don't care!

PROSECUTE-HER: But it wasn't fair

ANDREA: So what?!
Fuck cares if it's fair or not, you lose your head during a game, you got nothing left.
Refs don't catch every penalty so that gives you the right to make ten more? Why, because you're angry? No. No! Shit's not fair so you play like shit? NO.
Everything, everything has been an excuse with this team since day fucking one. I don't know what's going on with all of you but you know what I saw tonight? A mess. Eighteen little girls skating for themselves, slipping around the track like a bowl of sloppy noodles.
We're supposed to be the best. The best don't make excuses.

DIAZ: Yo, we WON.

ANDREA: Was the game entertaining? Yeah, sure was. A real nail-biter, just like Friday Night Fucking Lights, it was great.
But did you win?
No.
You didn't.
None of you won. You all lost. Big time.

(ANDREA leaves. The rest of the girls look around awkwardly. PROSECUTE-HER slams her shit to the ground.)

PROSECUTE-HER: Fuck her.

ANNA: Shit.

(MOUSE walks over to PROSECUTE-HER and comforts her but PROSECUTE-HER kinda brushes her off her so she leaves her alone.)

DIAZ: So. Who's going to the After Party?

ANNA: After that?

MOUSE: I need it more than ever after that.

HOT FLASH: She wasn't wrong, you know.

LIZZIE: Yes she was.
She was wrong about everything.

HOT FLASH: Nobody did listen to her –

JOY: She was making bad calls.

HOT FLASH: You think?

JOY: For sure.

ANNA: You going to the party, Flash?

HOT FLASH: I ain't going tonight, I gotta get home to Ronnie.

DIAZ: Imma be drowning myself in alcohol. Imma drink so much, it'll be running in my veins like instead of blood.

LIZZIE: I think that's called alcoholism.

DIAZ: Anna?

ANNA: Yeah, no, that's pretty much the definition of alcohol-ism.

DIAZ: Shut up.

MOUSE: Alcoholism would be a great derby name.

ANNA: How?

MOUSE: Ellie-Cohlism

DIAZ: No.

PROSECUTE-HER: Allie-Colism

ANNA: There it is

MOUSE: You're like master of the names.

PROSECUTE-HER: I'll add that to my resume.

ANNA: What about you, Joy? Going to the Party?

JOY: I don't think so –

LIZZIE: Seriously?

JOY: Where's it at, again?

LIZZIE: What's wrong, Jersey, you worried about getting home?

JOY: Kinda, I haven't heard from Michelle-

DIAZ: She probably assumes you're going.

JOY: I guess.

MOUSE: Come on

ANNA: Yeah, it was your first game.

LIZZIE: And we did win, contrary to the popular belief.

JOY: All right. I'll go.

MOUSE: Great!

PROSECUTE-HER: Yeah, great.

MOUSE: Oh, come on, cheer up!

HOT FLASH: Yeah, she yelled at all of us

MOUSE: Don't make me sing, I'll start to sing

DIAZ: Oh my god, I think she's serious

MOUSE: I am serious!

PROSECUTE-HER: Stop –

MOUSE: Who's the leader of the club, made for you and me?

PROSECUTE-HER: Oh my god, stop!

(MOUSE and PROSECUTE-HER exit, followed by ANNA and DIAZ.)

JOY: You coming?

LIZZIE: Yeah, I'll be a minute.
See you there, Rook.

(JOY leaves. LIZZIE is getting into street clothes, trying to look cute. ANDREA enters.)

LIZZIE: Forgot something?

ANDREA: You've gotta give me a break

LIZZIE: I didn't ask to be on this stupid team.

ANDREA: You have the shittiest attitude

LIZZIE: Guess I won't be winning Miss. Congeniality

ANDREA: Are you just doing this to torture me? Or do you really not trust me?

LIZZIE: How can I trust you, Drea? How?
Rompiste mi corazon

ANDREA: Don't do the Spanish thing

LIZZIE: No, I can't trust you.

ANDREA: I need to be able to coach you

LIZZIE: I shoulda never got switched to this team.

ANDREA: Don't say that

LIZZIE: Fine, I'll say whatever you want me to say.

ANDREA: I wish.

LIZZIE: How am I supposed to trust a coach who throws a shit fit when we win –

ANDREA: How'm I supposed to trust a team that don't listen–

LIZZIE: I took a risk. Sometimes you gotta take a risk. Right? Make sense? Not to you, never to you, you never wanted to take a risk your whole life. You can't, not even if you tried.

ANDREA: That's not true –

LIZZIE: Couldn't take a risk on us. Right? Couldn't trust us. So how'm I supposed to know you're doing right by the team.

ANDREA: You gotta separate –

LIZZIE: Nah, man, nah because I'm the one who lost, I'm the one who ended up alone. I don't even got the team because I gotta come here and see your scowling face and listen to your voice and remember the way you looked when you was waking up in the morning and no I can't separate it, it's too much to ask.

(LIZZIE starts to leave.)

ANDREA: What about Joy?

LIZZIE: The fuck about her

ANDREA: I ain't blind.

LIZZIE: Dunno what you're talking about

ANDREA: She make the team more bearable for you?

LIZZIE: Shut up

ANDREA: You gonna let her break your heart, too?

LIZZIE: You want me to bend down and kiss your ass in front of the other girls, because I won't do it. I don't believe a call you makin, I ain't gonna let it slide by. Don't go bringing Joy into this shit because she don't concern it. Aight?

ANDREA: Be careful, Lizzie.
You play too reckless, you're not the only one who gonna get hurt.

(ANDREA leaves. LIZZIE stands for a moment, collecting herself. The sound of bass music comes as the scene transforms into -)

64

Scene IX

(The After Party. This scene is set to music, bass pumping blood thumping music. It is choreographed, even though women are not on skates, it should almost feel like they could be. Dialgoue should be soaked up by the music.
SQUEAKY MOUSE and PROSECUTE-HER are joking around with DIAZ and ANNA. JOY is just standing around awkwardly. A new song comes on.)

DIAZ: That's my jam!

(She starts dancing by herself. MOUSE joins in, really goofily. They're all dancing together, laughing, it should look like a fucking blast.
JOY is looking around. MOUSE grabs her and starts to play-fully dance with her.)

MOUSE: Loosen up!

(JOY starts to get slightly more into it.
LIZZIE enters. She watches JOY. She walks to the other side of the bar, not dancing, just watching. She heads over to JOY. Starts dancing with her.
MICHELLE enters. She looks around.
MICHELLE spots JOY. Heads to her. JOY is having a really fun time by now. You can tell it by her smile.
MICHELLE touches her shoulder, JOY spins around and grabs her in a hug, gives her a quick kiss and tries to dance with her.
MICHELLE starts dancing with JOY. They're having a blast together. LIZZIE tries to start dancing with JOY again but JOY and MICHELLE break away and dance together. LIZZIE just watches.
MICHELLE kisses JOY and starts to pull her away. Note – it's not important that the following dialogue is heard, this is for the actors, it should be obvious that MICHELLE and JOY are fighting but the audience doesn't need to hear the details of what they're saying.)

JOY: Wait, I'm not ready -

MICHELLE: It's late

JOY: I know but –

MICHELLE: Come on, I gotta get home

JOY: Wait!

(She lets go.)

JOY: Dance with me

MICHELLE: I did –

JOY: More

MICHELLE: I'm tired

JOY: I won!
   Let's celebrate.

MICHELLE: Fine. You stay, I'm going.

JOY: Just stay –

MICHELLE: No. No. Whatever, no.

(MICHELLE leaves. JOY starts to follow her out but LIZZIE comes from behind her and starts to dance with her again. JOY keeps looking back but LIZZIE gets her to keep looking at her. They dance together. The music gets louder, so loud it almost sounds like the roar of the crowd.
Lights dim and the music falls away until the sound of a whistle.
Blackout.)

Scene X

(LIZZIE's tattoo shop. She's sitting there, reading a magazine. JOY enters.)

JOY: I'm here

LIZZIE: Holy shit, you didn't wuss out

JOY: I told you I wouldn't

LIZZIE: Fuck

*(They do a handshake thing.
JOY points to her back.)*

JOY: Right here.

LIZZIE: Yeah?

JOY: Yeah.

LIZZIE: Cool, let me just get my shit together.

(LIZZIE gets up, starts tracing the design onto carbon paper.)

(JOY looks around the shop.)

JOY: You made all these?

LIZZIE: No, fucking elves did.
Yeah, I did it.
This is my shop, it's only me.

JOY: That's actually impressive

LIZZIE: What are you, new? Yeah, it's impressive, I'm fucking impressive.
So. What's your girl think?

67

JOY: She doesn't know.

LIZZIE: You serious?

JOY: Yeah. It's my skin.

LIZZIE: Yeah. It's your skin.

(She holds up the drawing.)

LIZZIE: This's what you want, right?

JOY: That's the one

LIZZIE: Good. Get your ass in the chair.

(She gets in the chair.)

LIZZIE: Take off your top

JOY: Oh. Right.

(She takes off her top while LIZZIE takes out a Bic razor.)

JOY: The fuck you're doing with that?

LIZZIE: Calm down, I just gotta shave you

JOY: You have to fucking what me?

LIZZIE: Yo, I have to shave the spot Imma be working on, it's
    normal, Google it.

JOY: There's no hair there -

LIZZIE: You trust me?

JOY: Yeah, I mean that's why I came to you.

(LIZZIE is pleased. She shaves her.)

LIZZIE: You got beautiful skin

JOY: Nah
　　　Yeah?

(She puts the stencil on her during the following.)

LIZZIE: Yeah. Some people come in with scarred up skin,
real rough and gnarled, like the trunk've a tree. The ink
don't take.
　　　But your skin's soft.
　　　Real soft.
　　　I like it.

(She readies the tattoo gun, turns it on.)

JOY: Wait

LIZZIE: What?

JOY: Is it gonna hurt?

LIZZIE: Yeah.

JOY: Shit.

LIZZIE: But it'll feel good.

JOY: Good?

LIZZIE: It'll tickle.
　　　Like a thousand angel wings flapping against your back

JOY: Don't lie.

LIZZIE: It's a good hurt. Hurt can feel good sometimes, right?
Like how derby can knock the wind outta you but you get up
and just keep going. Right? Like when your muscles are so
sore you can't even move. Like when your body is covered
with sweat and bruises and they're ugly but also kinda beautiful because they're your bruises, you know?

69

JOY: Sure.

LIZZIE: You nervous?

JOY: No.

LIZZIE: It's okay.
To be nervous.
You don't gotta be brave with me.
You just gotta be you
with me
You ready?

JOY: Ok.

(LIZZIE starts the tattoo. JOY grimaces, LIZZIE stops it.)

LIZZIE: You okay?

JOY: Yeah, yeah, ow fuck.

LIZZIE: Maybe I shouldn't

JOY: No, no, it's okay.
Just
Talk to me, distract me
Please?

LIZZIE: Sure, ok

(Starts again.)

LIZZIE: Just lean into the pain.
Let it wrap around your brain,
It'll start to feel like a hug

JOY: A hug

LIZZIE: Sure. So.
Joy Ride.
It suits you better than your name.

JOY: Yeah?

LIZZIE: Yeah, for sure. Joy's gotta be a hard name to live up to, right? I mean, it's like a NOUN, you know? Like a real word, that's crazy. You either gotta go Wednesday Adams with it or become a fuckin' cheerleader, there's no wiggle room. And you definitely ain't neither of those.
But a Joy Ride, that's different. Because joy rides ain't all happiness, not really. It's intensity. It's going as fast as possible without crashing. Zooming across the highway, zoom, zoom, zoom.

(JOY laughs.)

JOY: You're crazy.

LIZZIE: Nah, I just like it when you smile. You turn into a whole other person.

(She continues the tattoo.)

LIZZIE: You want me to stop?

JOY: No.
You don't seem like much of a Lizzie.

LIZZIE: My name ain't Lizzie. Not really.

JOY RIDE: No?

LIZZIE: Nah. It's just my Derby Name.
After the Lizzies. You know, the gang in The Warriors?
Waaarriorsss…come out to PLAAA-AAAYYY
No?
Nothing?
Well, it's a movie. A cult classic, actually. And it's about a bunch of different gangs in the City and they're all after this one gang 'cause they think they killed this guy – whatever, you gotta watch it, but there's this one gang of women –

only one – and they called themselves The Lizzies. So that's where it comes from.

JOY RIDE: That's deep.

LIZZIE: Right?
But nobody gets the reference. So I don't correct them. It's cool.

JOY RIDE: So what's your real name?

LIZZIE: I don't tell nobody.

JOY RIDE: Right.

(Beat.)

LIZZIE: Marisol.

JOY RIDE: Yeah?

LIZZIE: Yeah.

JOY RIDE: That's-

LIZZIE: It's too heavy,

JOY RIDE: Beautiful.

LIZZIE: Nah.
Yeah?

JOY: Yeah.
I mean, I guess.

LIZZIE: Shut up.

(Quiet for a moment.)

LIZZIE: It was my mother's name.
Marisol.
It's like wearing her shadow on my back.
I hate it.

JOY: You okay?

LIZZIE: Yeah.

JOY: You don't have to be brave with me.

LIZZIE: Shut up

JOY: No, really.
You don't.

(Silence but for the tattoo gun.)

LIZZIE: How are you doing?

JOY: Fine.

LIZZIE: You want me to stop?

JOY: No. But
when does it start feeling like a hug?

LIZZIE: When you start embracing the pain.

JOY: Yeah, of course.

(Pause.)

LIZZIE: I'll hug you.
After this is all over.

JOY: Sure.

LIZZIE: I could kiss your skin.
Too.

(No words from Joy.)

LIZZIE: I bet it tastes nice.
   Too.
   I bet it tastes like salt from your sweat.
   I bet you taste good.
   Do you want me to stop?

(Buzzing.)

JOY: No.
   Don't stop.

LIZZIE: I could run my lips up and down your neck.
   My lips are like butterfly wings, flapping up and down your
   neck.
   I could run my hands up and down your thighs
   My fingers dancing up and down your thigh
   Up and down your thigh until
   They run around the side and slowly
   So slowly crawl
   Up

JOY: Stop

(She turns off the tattoo gun.
They sit there in silence for a moment.)

LIZZIE: You okay?

JOY: Yeah.
   Yeah, no, I'm fine.
   It was just
   hurting.

LIZZIE: You want me to -?

JOY: Just
   finish the tattoo.

LIZZIE: Sure.
   Sure, I'll just

(She turns the gun back on.

End of Act I.)

Act II

Scene I

(Dance sequence – much like a training montage, set to music. The sequence then goes into the locker room, after practice. The women are getting out of their gear. DIAZ suddenly enters. She throws her helmet into a locker.)

ANNA: Yo, Diaz, calm down.

DIAZ: This is bullshit.

HOT FLASH: What the fuck happened?

ANNA: Are you okay?

DIAZ: Don't even touch me right now, okay

JOY: What's up, Diaz?

DIAZ: Especially you, stay the fuck away

LIZZIE: The fuck's your problem?

DIAZ: How you gonna sit there and act like you don't know, you're the Captain of this goddamm team and you telling me you don't fucking know?

LIZZIE: No, I don't fucking know so abre tu boca y digame.

(ANDREA enters.)

ANDREA: Diaz, come on, we'll talk about it -

DIAZ: No. There ain't nothing to say to you, Andrea.

PROSECUTE-HER: What happened?

DIAZ: Rookie took my spot.

JOY: What?

ANDREA: I was gonna tell you all -
Yes, yes, I'm gonna be jamming Lizzie, Anna and Joy on
Saturday.

(There's a surprised silence in the room.)

JOY: Me?

ANDREA: Did I stutter?

JOY: No.

DIAZ: Bitch took my place

LIZZIE: Yo, watch your mouth, okay

DIAZ: Getting special treatment because she your pet

LIZZIE: Shut the fuck up

DIAZ: Deja la mierda, es porque estas acostandote con ella

LIZZIE: Calla tu maldita boca, puta

ANNA: Whoa whoa

(ANNA holds DIAZ back, JOY grabs LIZZIE.)

DIAZ: You just don't like it 'cause I'm calling you out pero tu
sabes que, everybody see it, es que nadie tiene los cajones
para decirte.

ANDREA: Stop it, STOP IT HEY if you don't stop it I'll cut
you both from the team.

(They stop but barely.)

LIZZIE: No tuve nada que ver con eso so shut up!

ANDREA: All right, that's it, ten laps, both of you!

DIAZ: No

ANDREA: Go

DIAZ: Vete pa' la mierda. You can just take me out like that, putting me on the sidelines? Nah, yo soy mejor que eso siempre ha sido mejor que eso.
I'm out.

(DIAZ goes slamming out of the locker room, still in her gear and skates. ANNA follows.)

ANDREA: It'll be all right. Just...get cleaned up. We gotta be outta here in fifteen.

(ANDREA leaves.)

HOT FLASH: The fuck was all that about

JOY: Guess she won't be needing a ride.

MOUSE: Maybe it's her shark week

JOY: What?

PROSECUTE-HER: She's on the rag.

JOY: Oh.

LIZZIE: Oh, please, don't do that, don't go calling period time of the month bullshit, no. Sometimes bitches are just bitches

MOUSE: Don't say that

LIZZIE: What, too R rated for your virgin ears?

MOUSE: You on the rag, too?

LIZZIE: No –

MOUSE: Then shut up.

HOT FLASH: I think we all might be tired. Right?

MOUSE: Sure. That must be it.

HOT FLASH: I'm ready to go home.

PROSECUTE-HER: Me too

MOUSE: Yeah, I think I'll take the train tonight.

JOY: Okay.

MOUSE: See ya.

(PROSECUTE-HER AND MOUSE leave.)

HOT FLASH: I gotta smoke.
      Meet you by the car?

JOY: Sure.

HOT FLASH
      Great.

(She leaves. It's just JOY and LIZZIE.)

LIZZIE: So. No pressure or anything.

JOY: Yeah, I was getting too much sleep anyway.

LIZZIE: Tensions just get high. Don't think about it, Diaz'll
   cool down. Besides, you'll be great.

JOY: What'd she say?

LIZZIE: Nothing.

JOY: Didn't sound like nothing.

LIZZIE: It's nothing –

JOY: Sounded like she was accusing me? Of something?

LIZZIE: Don't worry about it

JOY: Why won't you tell me?

(LIZZIE considers. She's about to say something when HOT FLASH comes in.)

HOT FLASH: Hey, you comin or what?

(LIZZIE leaves. JOY is by herself.)

The sound of the crowd again, an announcer announces.)

ANNOUNCER: Number 1101, you'll know her when you see her, it's Diaz de los Muertos!

(DIAZ comes out. She's in a graveyard. There is a physical headstone she talks to throughout.
She lights a candle. Puts it on the grave. Sits in front of it.)

DIAZ: I would've brought you flowers but. It's too cold out. Today.
The candle should warm you up.
All these other graves, they got people showing off, but it ain't fair for flowers to freeze. Right?
(She lies her head down on the ground, in front of the head-stone. Breathes.)
Can you feel this?
Can you hear me?
You always said I was too loud. Can you still hear me? Jay?
Sometimes I look into the wind, trying to find flashes and shit that I can tear open and step inside, like you were some-where I can find.

Stupid, right?

Whatever, Jay.

(She sits up.)

Mama says we should forgive the motherfucker for what he did to you.

What'd'you think? Should I do that?

Oh wait, you're dead. I think that answers that.

(She stands. Turns to leave.)

Tulips. In the Spring, I will bring you tulips

Te lo juro.

(She kisses the grave. Leaves.)

Scene II

(JOY and MICHELLE's bedroom. They've just come back from grocery shopping.)

JOY: Shit. You know what we forgot to get? The peas. The frozen peas that we both like?

MICHELLE: Shit.

JOY: I'm gonna have to go back

MICHELLE: Fuck the peas, stay here.

JOY: No, I better go

MICHELLE: Come on, I never see you anymore.

JOY: I know. Those double shifts are killing me.

MICHELLE: Come here. Let me give you a massage.

JOY: I only have like an hour before I gotta go.

MICHELLE: So spend it with me.

JOY: But the peas –

MICHELLE: I'll get the peas.

JOY: All right.

(She sits next to MICHELLE on the bed and she holds her.)

MICHELLE: All right. So I've been thinking – and don't say no until you hear it, okay?

JOY: Okay.

MICHELLE: So they really like you at the Foot Locker

JOY: I know. I'm like maxed out on time I'm supposed to be there.

MICHELLE: So why don't you ask for a promotion?

JOY: A promotion?
A promotion to what?

MICHELLE: To something more senior there.

JOY: I don't think so.

MICHELLE: Like if they have an openings, just tell them to keep you in mind -

JOY: I just – no.

MICHELLE: Joy, I'm worried. I've already applied to like fifty jobs and signed up with 9 temp agencies and nobody's called me

JOY: You just started

MICHELLE: I needed something like yesterday.
I don't know what we can do, rent's due in ten days

JOY: That's what savings are for

MICHELLE: Yeah but we can't keep going like that, you know? We got so much to pay, there's gas, there's food, there's so much more –

JOY: Michelle, come on, I mean, we're going to figure it out

MICHELLE: You keep saying that but then you don't say how–

JOY: All right, let me just get through the season, okay?

MICHELLE: That's too long

JOY: Fine, let me just get through the game

MICHELLE: You have a game?

JOY: Yeah, tomorrow

MICHELLE: Oh.

JOY: You forgot?

MICHELLE: I just didn't realize
  I'm sorry

JOY: No, it's fine let's just stop talking about it.
  Okay?

MICHELLE: Okay.

JOY: You owe me a massage.

MICHELLE: Right. Right.

(She kisses the top of JOY's head. Starts to massage her shoulders, JOY recoils.)

JOY: Fuck

MICHELLE: What, what, what I do-

JOY: It's nothing, nothing

MICHELLE: No, what is it? Please, tell me

JOY: It's stupid,

MICHELLE: Another derby wound?

JOY: Nah, my own doing
  Gotta tattoo.

MICHELLE: What?

JOY: Yeah. Forgot to tell you.

MICHELLE: You got a tattoo without telling me?

JOY: Yeah

MICHELLE: Oh.

JOY: Yeah, it was pretty intense.

MICHELLE: I bet.

JOY: Like, it's not that it hurt, really…I mean, it did, it hurt a lot, but it was a hurt you can get used to. The longer it went on, it was like my mind started buzzing. And even though it was tearing into my skin, it felt like it was worth it. I loved it. Can't wait to get another.
You're not talking.

MICHELLE: What's it of?

JOY: My name

MICHELLE: You hate your name

JOY: Not that name.
Joy Ride.

MICHELLE: Oh.

JOY: Yeah, see, you can see it, here

(She shows MICHELLE.)

JOY: It's nice, right? Clean lines or whatever.

MICHELLE: It's… something.

JOY: You hate it.

MICHELLE: I didn't know you were thinking about getting a tattoo.

JOY: I didn't realize you'd wanna know

MICHELLE: I mean, it's a tattoo, that's pretty huge, it's kinda huge to not tell me

JOY: Yeah, maybe if I was sixteen and you were my mom –

MICHELLE: No, it is, a big deal, a million things could've gone wrong

JOY: You sound like a Huffington Post article right now

MICHELLE: People get diseases from dirty needles

JOY: I'm not a fuckin' tourist, Michelle, I'm not going to go to a Canal Street hole in the wall that sells fish in the front and does 50 dollar tattoos in the back

MICHELLE: So how much was it?

JOY: Don't start.

MICHELLE: I'm not starting anything

JOY: It was free

MICHELLE: Free

JOY: Just say what you're thinking

MICHELLE: I am

JOY: No, no you're not, you're dancing around it

MICHELLE: Fine, where'd you get that fucking tattoo, Joy?

JOY: Somebody I know gave it to me. In her legit, well lit, clean needle'd shop.

MICHELLE: Her?

JOY: What's that mean

MICHELLE: Who's Her?

JOY: No, what are you trying to say with it like that Her

MICHELLE: Nothing. Nothing.

JOY: Lizzie, she gave it to me, okay?

MICHELLE: Lizzie?

JOY: Lizzie Lightning

MICHELLE: Oh, right.

JOY: For all the rides.

MICHELLE: Great.

JOY: You mad right now?

MICHELLE: No

JOY: All right.
    I'm gonna go get the peas.
    (Starts to leave.)

MICHELLE: Why that?

JOY: Why what?

MICHELLE: Joy Ride.

JOY RIDE: 'Cause that's my name

MICHELLE: Derby.
It's your derby name, it's not your real name, it's not even
your nickname, it's just a name you gave yourself when you
started the team.

JOY: Okay, wow.

MICHELLE: What, it's true, I think it's a huge mistake,
HUGE. You were never Joy Ride before and now you're
gonna be stuck with it on your skin for the rest of your life.

JOY: That's the idea

MICHELLE: But you're not going to be doing derby forever

JOY: Says who?

MICHELLE: Seriously?
You're not.

JOY: You sound like you're jealous

MICHELLE: I am not

JOY: You wish you had this, you WISH you had something to
live and die by, you don't know what that's like

MICHELLE: Really. Because I would live and die by you.

JOY: That's not what I meant

MICHELLE: I would live and die by us.

JOY: So would I –

MICHELLE: I'm glad, Joy, I'm glad you found your thing, the
thing you can finally live and die by, I'm so glad. Congratulations.

(MICHELLE gets up.)

JOY: I don't get why you're so upset about this, it's a tattoo, it's a stupid tattoo, I thought you'd understand, you used to be an artist!

(Beat.)

MICHELLE: What did you say?

JOY: I didn't mean -

MICHELLE: No, no you're right. I used to be an artist.
I used to be an artist and we used to live in Brooklyn and I used to think I couldn't live or breathe without making art, it all just flowed out of me, like breathing but guess what, it turns out that I can live without it, I had to learn how to breathe without it because I couldn't do it forever and now I'm not a fucking artist.
Thanks, Joy.

JOY: Come on, Michelle, you know I didn't mean it like that

MICHELLE: I don't know anything right now

JOY: Don't leave, stay with me

MICHELLE: I don't want to.

JOY: Then let me go with you

MICHELLE: No. Just let me…I need to breathe, I need to go somewhere I need, I need to get the peas.

(She leaves. JOY doesn't follow her.)

JOY: Shit.

(Lights turn pink and happy, bouncy music begins to play as the Announcer announces.)

Scene III

ANNOUNCER: We'll keep this short and sweet, it's Number Five point Oh, here she comes, it's Squeaky Mouse!

(She comes out wearing a graduation cap and gown, a remix of pomp and circumstance playing. She's practicing her valedictorian speech.)

SQUEAKY MOUSE: Friends, Romans, Countrymen, lend me your ears.
We did it!!! We're fucking graduating!!
What?
What'd'you mean I can't say it like that?
It's graduation day, who gives a shit what I'm even saying, nobody's even listening.
Can you stop rolling your eyes at me? Fine, I'll just read it from –
(Clears her throat)
Today we graduate.
You know, all of my life, I've been short. No, like, my whole life. I was always the runty kid. The slowest. I bet you think I'm gonna say it made me invisible. But it didn't. It made me small. In everyone's eyes. Like an ant. A bug that could just be swatted away. It made my heart small, shrivel up in my chest. Made me look at this world full of giants, scared. Like an ant.
But then, I started doing roller derby. And a crazy thing happened. I got taller. Instantly. Literally, three inches. And I started knocking bitches – women – down, and getting knocked down and getting back up again. I'm short, but I'm fast, and I'm powerful and I got good balance and – best of all – I don't give up. So now, even when I take my skates off, I don't shrink no more.
There's gonna be times in our lives, outside the womb of college – Can I say womb? okay – Outside the womb of college where we're gonna feel less than. We're gonna feel short. But it's just an illusion – a trick of the giants around us. Don't let nobody take away your voice – make it louder.

Don't let nobody step on you. Trip them instead. And don't let nobody shrivel your heart. Do what you gotta to make it grow.

So how about that?

That was good, right?

Yeah, I know it was.

(The sound of a game. Movement. This should be choreographed to the Commentators' Commentary but shouldn't be literal.

ANNA, SQUEAKY MOUSE, LIZZIE and JOY come out in their colors, HOT FLASH, ANDREA, PROSECUTE-HER and DIAZ will play girls from the opposing team.)

COMMENTATOR: Lizzie Lightning at the end of another Power Jam, you know what they say, you can't contain her, you can only detain her!

Looks like they're coming around the bend, Steamboat Millie from the Bronx Toxins trying to break her way through the Scallywags' pack, Lizzie Lightning, Anna-Stecia and Squeaky Mouse working together to make that wall they're so famous for, Joy Ride also struggling to get through the Toxins' defense

Looks like Joy is trying to pass the star, trying to get that star to Lizzie which would transfer the jam to her

But it looks like Steamboat Millie has used the distraction to break free, she is the lead jammer right now and Lizzie has successfully gotten the star but she's at the back of the pack and there's no way she –

NO WAY, she's just jumped the apex and –

(Lights change to red. This should be choreographed to have the feeling of the commentator's words but shouldn't be taken literally.)

COMMENTATOR: Oh, shit oh no

It looks like Lizzie tried to jump the apex and collided into Squeaky Mouse who has gone down, face first onto the track and

It looks like the ladies can't stop themselves, they're all col-
liding and skating over her and
We need the medic has somebody got
The rest of the players have taken a knee and
It looks like there's a few down
But Squeaky Mouse isn't moving, she's not moving

(The sound of an ambulance goes into.)

Scene IV

(The locker room after the game.   The girls are subdued.
MOUSE is missing.
ANDREA enters. PROSECUTE-HER shoots up.)

PROSECUTE-HER: Is she going to be okay?

ANDREA: Could've been worse

ANNA: That's not an answer

JOY: What's the damage?

ANDREA: She's…going to be out for the rest of the season
  Broken nose

HOT FLASH: And?

PROSECUTE HER: Don't play with us, coach, I saw her ankle, I saw it, it didn't even look like an ankle, the bone was
  sticking out her skin

ANDREA: Yeah, yes, her ankle got fucked. She's gonna need
  surgery to get it…to fix it. But she's young. She could-

PROSECUTE-HER: Where'd they take her?

ANDREA: Coney Island Hospital.

PROSECUTE-HER: Fuck

DIAZ: That shit was crazy

HOT FLASH: The way she just –

PROSECUTE-HER: Don't say

ANNA: So much blood

PROSECUTE-HER: I just skated right over her

JOY: Goddammit.

PROSECUTE-HER: I couldn't stop and I skated right over her.

LIZZIE: I've taken a skate to the face before. That's how I lost that tooth, she'll be fine.

PROSECUTE-HER: That's all you have to say?

LIZZIE: What else should I say?
Yeah, she'll be fine, she's going to be fine, this is what the game is it's rough. Right? Can't take it, don't play it.
Excuse me for being optimistic.

PROSECUTE-HER: Yeah, excuse you, if it wasn't for you she probably wouldn't have gotten hurt

LIZZIE: Accidents happen

PROSECUTE-HER: This shit didn't have to happen, you were playing too rough
You were both playing too rough

LIZZIE: No such thing

PROSECUTE-HER: There's obviously such a thing, Squeaky Mouse wiped out

LIZZIE: I jumped the apex like I've jumped the apex a hundred times before

PROSECUTE-HER: You shouldn't have jumped it, the pack was too close

LIZZIE: I thought I could make it

JOY: Maybe you shouldn't have jumped it

LIZZIE: Excuse me?

JOY: I shouldn't have passed you the star, I panicked

LIZZIE: Maybe I shouldn't've jumped the apex and you shouldn't've given me the star and the wind blew in the wrong fucking direction, does it make a difference, is it gonna make the accident not happen? NO. Am I still gonna play like that? YES.

PROSECUTE-HER: You don't even care

LIZZIE: You're right, I don't, I don't give a shit because I did what I had to do and we won the game

PROSECUTE-HER: I'm sick of your shit, Lizzie, you're a fucking accident waiting to happen.

LIZZIE: You wanna go, we can go right now

PROSECUTE-HER: Sure, let's go

(They get in each other's faces, ANDREA gets in the middle.)

ANDREA: All right, enough, ENOUGH
Stop throwing blame around, accidents happen, it's part of the game!

PROSECUTE-HER: It didn't have to happen

LIZZIE: Yeah because you're such a good skater

PROSECUTE-HER: You know what, I'm done, fuck this shit. FUCK IT. I'm done. I'm not going to let my shit get compromised because of a roller-skating diva bitch and her lapdog.

JOY: Yo

PROSECUTE-HER: That's all you are, Joy and you know it, ever since you got on this team you've done nothing but lick up Lizzie's shit.
You both weren't playing with us, you were playing by yourselves, you didn't give a shit about anybody else out there. It was the Joy and Lizzie show. And I'm sick of it.

(She leaves.)

LIZZIE: Chicken shit.

ANDREA: Chill, Lizzie.

(Beat.)

DIAZ: What are we gonna do?

HOT FLASH: Down two players

ANDREA: We're gonna figure it out.
I'll figure it out.
We're in the play offs. That's a good thing. Hold onto that.
Good game, ladies. Good game.

(She leaves. The ladies put their stuff on.)

JOY: Lizzie

(LIZZIE leaves, angrily. JOY is left alone.)

Scene V

(The bedroom. MICHELLE is sitting on the bed. JOY enters.)

MICHELLE: Hey.

JOY: Hey.
  Sorry I'm late

MICHELLE: It's okay

JOY: Game ran over

MICHELLE: It's fine
  How'd you do?

JOY: We won.

MICHELLE: Congratulations.

JOY: There was an accident – one of the players got messed up

MICHELLE: Shit. Is she going to be okay?

JOY: Probably, kinda, I dunno.

MICHELLE: Can you sit?

JOY: I was going to take a shower.

MICHELLE: You didn't shower after?

JOY: No time.

MICHELLE: I just
  have to tell you something,

JOY: Can it wait like five minutes?
  I really need a shower.

MICHELLE: Sure.

JOY: Great.

(She starts to leave.   MICHELLE speaks, stops her in her tracks.)

MICHELLE: I got a job.

JOY: Oh. That's great

MICHELLE: Yeah

JOY: You can stop worrying now
   Congratulations.
   I'm just gonna -

MICHELLE: Do you want to marry me?

JOY: You asking?

MICHELLE: I mean, eventually.
   Do you want to marry me?

JOY: Michelle

MICHELLE: It's in Oregon.

JOY: What is?

MICHELLE: The job. It's in Oregon.

JOY: You serious right now?

MICHELLE: For a startup out there.

JOY: What's the job?

MICHELLE: VP of –

JOY: So not designing

MICHELLE: Yeah but –

JOY: Same shit you've been miserable doing here

MICHELLE: It's not shit –

JOY: You're not happy doing it

MICHELLE: It's a job. And it's more money than I would be making here. And it's a lower cost of living. We can save up for a house. A real house, not some tiny, squashed apartment.
Listen, we don't have to leave for two months, okay? The season'll be over by then and Portland has derby teams, too, so I figure you can go to school, just a couple of classes here and there during the day and then still have the chance to do derby in the evening,–

JOY: In Oregon

MICHELLE: It's exciting
Don't you think it's exciting?

JOY: I tell you I wanna move back to Brooklyn and you take that as Let's move across the fucking country?

MICHELLE: Portland is the new Brooklyn

JOY: Nobody says that

MICHELLE: A lot of people say that

JOY: Portland isn't Brooklyn. It's the fucked up hipster infested artist run disaster that Brooklyn has become it's not real, it's not real Brooklyn, the team, that's real Brooklyn, that's my heartbeat, it's the blood that runs through my veins and you want to take it away from me, the last thing that I had that connected me to Brooklyn?

MICHELLE: Well what do you propose we do?

JOY: You don't give a shit what I wanna do

MICHELLE: What, you wanna move to Brooklyn and?
    Then what?
    Do roller derby AND?
    Then WHAT?

JOY: There's more to life than making money

MICHELLE: Sure, there's health insurance and retirement and

JOY: That's not it

MICHELLE: Yeah? What is there?
    Go ahead, enlighten me
(Expectant pause.)
    Go ahead,
    I'm waiting.

JOY: What, there were no jobs here you could get

MICHELLE: Do you know how many jobs I applied to? How
    many hundreds of jobs I applied to? And I got three inter-
    views, THREE. That's IT. What choice did I have, what
    did you want me to do?
    I'm trying to take care of things, I'm trying to make a future
    for us, what're you doing, what're you doing for us, for US,
    you don't give a shit about us, it's all about You
    It's always all about you

JOY: I'm not moving to Oregon

MICHELLE: Joy

JOY: And how the fuck could you think I would?
    Fuck that

MICHELLE: What's holding you here, really? We don't own
    a home, you don't have a real job -

JOY: I'm on the team

MICHELLE: Portland's got teams

JOY: Half assed teams

MICHELLE: Who cares, they're teams, aren't they?

JOY: I care

MICHELLE: Yeah, you care, that's all you care about

JOY: That's not true

MICHELLE: Oh yeah?
You don't give a shit about anything except for the team.
Ever since you got on, everything revolves around the team.
Everything revolves around them.

JOY: You're the one who wanted me to join!

MICHELLE: It's taken over your life, it's taken over our lives!
And what are you supposed to do with it? It's nothing, it's
NOTHING it's a hobby -

JOY: What did you think it would be, just something to get the
housewife outta the house?

MICHELLE: To get you to go and DO something, I thought
you'd wanna actually DO something with your life, I didn't
think everything would revolve around the team-

JOY: What else do you want from me, I picked up more shifts,
I'm on the team and what do you care about?
How can you just go back to doing the same shit

MICHELLE: Someone has to make money, someone has to
make the plans for the future, someone has to take care of
Us, you don't take care of Us, you don't give a shit about Us

JOY: Because you cut me out

MICHELLE: No I didn't

JOY: Remember when you did that thing on the highway?
  You turned garbage bags into angel wings and stapled them
  to highway signs in the middle of the night while I stood
  watch. I was your partner.
  I used to be your partner.
  What happened?

MICHELLE: I don't know.

JOY: And you come at me, acting like it's my fault you lost
  your job,

MICHELLE: I never said

JOY: acting like it's my fault you need to worry

MICHELLE: You don't worry!

JOY: acting like I'm nothing but a waste of space

MICHELLE: Sometimes I don't know whether or not you are!

(Pause.)

JOY: The fuck you just said

MICHELLE: Nothing, I didn't -

JOY: I am NOT A FUCKING WASTE OF SPACE.

(JOY starts packing.)

MICHELLE: I didn't mean – don't do that, stop it

JOY: You don't even know who I am

MICHELLE: Because you won't tell me

JOY: You don't listen to the answers!
No, I don't wanna go to college, yeah, I know I need to do something, no I don't know what it is, no I don't wanna be a manager of a fucking store, are you kidding me?

MICHELLE: Stop packing

JOY: No

MICHELLE: Seriously stop doing that

JOY: Leave me alone

MICHELLE: I didn't want it to go like this

JOY: How did you want it to go?

MICHELLE: Better than this
Please, can you just stop

JOY: I got nothing else to say to you

MICHELLE: Where do you think you're gonna go?

JOY: I don't know where the fuck I'm going, I'm going to just wander the streets until I find a gutter to lie down in

MICHELLE: Fine. Whatever, do whatever you want, I'm going to go to Portland, okay, I'm going to Portland and I'm going to be the Vice President of a startup and I just want you to come with me
Okay?

(JOY stands at the door.)

MICHELLE: Please don't go

JOY: You've done nothing but hate me since the minute I got on the team

MICHELLE: I don't hate you, I don't, I don't
Please.

JOY: I'm tired.
I'm so tired of you telling me what to do, telling me how to feel, what to think

MICHELLE: That's not what –

JOY: Yes it is.
It is.
I'm going.

(JOY leaves.)

Scene XVI

(The locker room. JOY is sleeping on a bench. ANDREA en-
ters, turning on the lights. JOY groans.)

ANDREA: Joy?

JOY: No.

ANDREA: What're you doing sleeping on the bench?

JOY: The floor was too cold.

ANDREA: You're not supposed to be here.

JOY: Yeah I know.
But I had nowhere else to go.

ANDREA: Everything okay?

JOY: Fine.
Got my skates. Got my gear. I'm fine.

ANDREA: You wanna tell me what's wrong?

JOY: Not really.

ANDREA: Okay. You wanna talk about sports or something?

JOY: No.

ANDREA: Okay.
Weather's been pretty interesting.

JOY: Right

ANDREA: Listen, I'm not really good at this, at the talking
one on one thing, I can tell there's something wrong but I
don't know how to coax it out of you and it's quite frankly
making me uncomfortable so Imma just go and get the track
set down so -

JOY: I don't know what I'm doing.

ANDREA: Oh. Nobody does.

JOY: That's not true.

ANDREA: I don't know what I'm doing.

JOY: I'm pretty sure you shouldn't be telling me that

ANDREA: Well I don't. I really don't. I think I know what I'm doing. Team's a mess. That's my fault. But Imma keep trying, you know? We're gonna figure it out together.

JOY: Why am I doing this

ANDREA: What?

JOY: This, this. Derby, my life, this.

ANDREA: You don't like it?

JOY: No, I love it. I really, really love it but what is it? It's nothing, it's getting me nowhere, who cares. Who cares?

ANDREA: You care
Isn't that enough?

JOY: No

ANDREA: The fuck you mean No, yes it is

JOY: It isn't

ANDREA: Lemme ask you something, when's the last time you did something because you wanted to do it?
Give me an answer.

JOY: I... don't know.

ANDREA: That's not an answer.

JOY: It's my answer.

ANDREA: Then it's a shitty answer. You should know what
  you want. And you shouldn't feel bad about wanting what
  you want.
  I've never done this before, coaching. It's different. Being
  on the outside looking in. Planning, training, talking to large
  groups of people, it's all hard. I miss skating. I miss playing. I wasn't even that good, but I loved it, I loved it so
  much. But my knees went – no more cartlidge. It runs in
  the family, has nothing to do with derby. I had to stop playing. It broke my heart, to walk away.
  But I couldn't just leave it. I couldn't just let it go. I love it
  too much to let it go. So I'll figure out a way to make it
  work because I have to. Derby is my heart. I can't just lose
  my heart. Not without a fight.
  Every time I come here, even if it's the shittiest day, even if
  I have women dropping off the team left and right, even if
  we keep on losing, every time I come here I choose to do it.
  I don't come here because I have to. I choose to come here.
  I choose to do this.
  Listen, the fact you care about this, that it makes you feel
  kindaf alive? That should mean something. Even if it's
  something you can't have, you should know that it means
  something. The fact that you care, that means something.
  The fact you want this. It means something.
  Doesn't it?

JOY: Thanks.

(ANDREA pats her on the back.)

ANDREA: That wasn't too bad, right?

JOY: Not at all.

ANDREA: Since you're here you can help me get the track
  down, yeah?

JOY: Yeah. Sure.

ANDREA: Good.

Scene XVI

(After practice. It is raining. LIZZIE and JOY are under an awning, watching.
It's
  awkward.)

JOY: You wanna make a run for it?

LIZZIE: To the car?

JOY: Yeah

LIZZIE: Don't wanna get my gear wet.

JOY: Yeah, me neither.
   It'll pass.

LIZZIE: Yeah, sure.

(Thunder.)

JOY: So. Are you gonna talk to me or what?

LIZZIE: I'm tired.

JOY: Okay.

(Thunder.)

LIZZIE: Why'd you do that? Take their side the other day.

JOY: I didn't take anyone's side.

LIZZIE: I thought you had my back.
   Nobody usually has my back. Except for you.

JOY: I'm sorry.

LIZZIE: Sure.

JOY: You gonna forgive me?

LIZZIE: It's whatever.

JOY: Okay.

(It keeps raining.)

JOY: It's pretty
   The rain.

LIZZIE: Pretty?

JOY: Yeah

LIZZIE: This shit?

JOY: What, you don't think it's pretty? Or like...cozy?

LIZZIE: Nah, I don't.

JOY: Okay.

(Beat.)

JOY: You ever dance in the rain?
   Like splashing in puddles and shit?

LIZZIE: Yeah, of course. I always did.

JOY: Me too.
   I used to jump in puddles, the bigger the better. Searching
   for a rabbithole or a way to get to Oz or Narnia. Neverland.
   Even Wonka's Chocolate Factory. Convinced myself that I
   could find a portal if I just jumped in the right one. A portal
   outta the City, into a crazy world of candy and princesses
   and talkin' animals.
   It's stupid now, though. Jumping in puddles. Childish.

LIZZIE: Yeah.

(They watch it rain. JOY suddenly jumps from under the awning and into a puddle.)

LIZZIE: HEY!

JOY: You gonna do something?

LIZZIE: Imma get soaked!

(JOY splashes in another puddle.)

JOY: You're already soaked

(LIZZIE runs out from underneath the awning and also begins to jump in puddles. Puddle after puddle after puddle. They're playing with one another. It's joy. Pure, uninhibited joy. Together.
They're laughing and breathless and getting each other soaked. JOY is trying to say something but she's laughing too hard to get it out.)

LIZZIE: I –

JOY: What?

(LIZZIE grabs her by the waist.)

JOY: What are you ...

(LIZZIE kisses JOY.
JOY hesitates
pushes her away, ending the kiss
They stare at one another like strangers for a moment before JOY moves towards the shelter of the awning.)

JOY: Stop it.

LIZZIE: Why?

JOY: Because! I don't want...no.

LIZZIE: Oh.

JOY: Yeah.

LIZZIE: I thought you wanted -

JOY: I don't.

LIZZIE: Okay

(She tries to get close to JOY but JOY walks away from her.)

LIZZIE: What, is this because of your girl?

JOY: Don't talk about my shit

LIZZIE: Your shitty girlfriend?

JOY: Shut the fuck up

LIZZIE: She don't see you, Joy, not the way I see you, I see you and I know you see me, too. I've never had anyone I could talk to about everything, you make me say things I didn't know about myself, and I make you happy, you can't even say that I don't, I do, I make you happy and I'll do anything to keep making you happy

JOY: Stop telling me what I want
Nobody knows what the fuck I want, nobody cares what I want.
Nobody.

LIZZIE: Please don't do this

JOY: I don't want you.

LIZZIE: Joy Ride

JOY: Don't call me that, Marisol.

(She starts to leave.)

LIZZIE: Hey. Hey! How the fuck'm I supposed to get home?

JOY: I don't know.

LIZZIE: Well I never would've fuckin' kissed you if I knew you'd just leave me stranded in the middle of nowhere.

JOY: You know, I used to think you were cool, and you are, you're so cool you're like ice and everything glides right off of you. Nothing sticks. No one can stick. You see something you want, you take it and you don't care what happens, as long as you get what you want. But I don't want you. I don't want you. I want to jump in puddles. I want to dance by myself in the rain, I want to run so fast my feet turn into wings and I fly headfirst into the sky! I don't want to be someone else's someone else, I want to know what it's like to be me.

(JOY leaves.
LIZZIE stands in the midst of the puddles that were just their playground, watching the water reflect lights from the night sky, rippling on the ground as thought the sky had fallen and is trapped. She kicks the water, watches as the sky crumples.)

LIZZIE: Ah, shit.
Shit.

Scene XVII

(The locker room during half time of the game. The girls come skating in. They're all really depressed. It is not going well. LIZZIE comes in angrily. Slams a locker door open. JOY follows.)

ANDREA: What was that out there?

ANNA: What?

ANDREA: You all stopped trying

DIAZ: We didn't

JOY: We did.

HOT FLASH: So what if we did?
    We're losing.

DIAZ: By over 100 points

LIZZIE: There's no way we can win.

JOY: So what?
    We don't play to win.
    We play because we have to.
    Right?

ANDREA: Right.

JOY: We don't just give up, throw it to the side and say surrender. We don't stop because we can't win, that's not why we play, we play to Play. We play to feed our souls, to keep going, we play for the love of the game, not for the score.
    Look around you. This locker room is full of your sisters. Your teammates. All of us, we all share one heartbeat and when one of us is out of whack, then we all go out of whack. That's when we lose not because of what the scoreboard

says, not because of what the officials are saying, but because we stopped trying.

We play until we can't go any more and then we push a little harder.

People spend their entire lives searching for something that they can fight for, and we all found it. We all have it.

So let's fight for the losing score. We're gonna fight until our hearts burst. And then go a little further. Because we love it. And anything you love, that's something worth fighting for.

(LIZZIE stands. She puts her hand in. Looks at everyone else.)

LIZZIE: Well?

(One by one each girl follows suit, putting her hand on top of LIZZIE's. JOY is the last one.)

JOY: Now. Let's go lose this bitch.

(The women release their hands in a wild scream, a scream of joy and ecstasy as they skate out to the rink.
And so the final dance sequence begins, losing the game.
It should be the most, unabashedly fun dance we've had so far.
Everyone dances together. Clear that everybody is losing the game.
Michelle joins the dance.
One by one, the women stop dancing, they go to the side, clapping or thumping their feet, like a heartbeat.
The heartbeat gets louder and louder as more and more of the women fall to the side, until it's just Michelle, Lizzie and Joy, until it's just Michelle and Joy.
until it's just Joy,
until the whistle blows which signals
the end of the game.)

End of play.

Made in the USA
San Bernardino, CA
01 March 2020